More t

by Jacob Lasher

This is a work of fiction. Any names or characters, businesses or places, events or incidents, are creations of the author's imagination.
Any resemblance to actual persons, living or dead, or actual events is purely coincidental. Or they could be completely true.

Copyright ©2019 Jacob Lasher

This book was written for all the people out there who are struggling with mental illness.

Many people don't understand this ongoing battle, and my hope is that <u>More to Life</u> will reach someone who needs to read it.

Maybe I can help open the eyes of those who aren't aware of how real the struggle is.

Even if I reach only one person, the effort will be worthwhile.

And if you or anyone you know needs help, please seek assistance right away.

There are phone numbers at the back of this book.

There is always a better option than to hurt yourself.

Stay safe!

-JL

4

PART ONE
cause and effect

Take Care

You need to take care of yourself,
Because you're all you have.

Love yourself;
Your body loves you.

Your skin repairs itself;
Your hair will grow back.

Thank your body for loving you.

Mask

Wearing a mask isn't that hard
When you're covered with scars.

Wearing a mask is easy to do
When you're running from the truth.

I wear mine every single day
And act like everything is normal.

But all of it is fake.

The Wolf

When we were young,
Mother pig brought home the big bad wolf.

But instead of blowing the house down,
He shut it down.

He went from calm to angry;
Holes in the wall became normal.

Three little pigs became three scared little kids,
While mother pig just watched.

Refill

When I was ten years old,
My stepfather beat me black and blue.

He broke my tooth.

I'd fight and struggle,
But what was the use?

I craved freedom from this life.

My mother stood there staring.
Tell me, why did you stop caring?

I was so consumed by the bullshit,
I forgot how to breathe.

I wanted to scar up my skin,
And I got curious with a little knife.

I never told;
I was terrified.

I wore baggy clothes to make myself less appealing,
Because my stepfather had something he was stealing.

I said *no please, I'll do anything,*
But he just laughed and said *you'll take what I bring.*

I made myself vomit so I would be thin,

Anything to feel accepted and adored.

I don't know why I did those things.
I'm still caught up in the past.

My sister meant everything,
But her life was on a string.

Ongoing pressures we couldn't endure -
We dealt with them every day.

Sometimes I wonder what for.

Now I take the medicine,
And then I do it again.

Will it make it better?

Refill, refill, refill.

Hide and Seek

I remember playing hide and seek in our backyard.

Feeling so safe, sheltered, and untouchable.
Running freely.

Nothing to worry about, nothing to fear.

Take me back to the days of hide and seek,
When things weren't as they are.

When I was innocent.

Do It Well

I don't know how you do it, but you do it well.
Channeling lies as if they were true.
Strangers sinking their teeth into your bloodlines.
And you act like it's a normal day.

I won't lie and pretend it's all right,
Because I've done that before, almost every night.
Swallowing lies like scraps at dinner time.
Breaking glasses, walking a thin line.

You sold us out as we waited in the clearance section,
And I was mocked because I had no direction.
I don't know how you process such thoughts, but you do.
You lie like a rhythm to your favorite tune.

Cavities in your molars, countryside dental care,
Stale potato chips, dirt roads in the middle of nowhere.
Empty beer cans, trashed on the secrets you feed.
They're not just white lies anymore.

Your heart is rotting like the poison apple
You should have baked into the pie.
You gave in to him completely.
You let us down.

I don't know how you did that,
But you did it well.

Glass House

Once upon a time,
I saw a shooting star in the November sky.
I made a wish,
And closed my ten-year-old eyes.

If only this house was made of glass,
Then you'd know why my mother's arm is in a cast.
If you could see that happen, you'd see it all,
If only there weren't any of these walls.

You could peek into the glass house
And see the monster I fear.
I've lived with these demons for eighteen years.
And no one wants to believe they're in the wrong.
A few thousand days wouldn't be that long.
I'll just follow my hazy mind, use vices to cope;
Find it all bittersweet, create distortions for hope.

I live in a glass house, this November 2005 house.
Everyone's staring, but they're not helping.
What's wrong with you people? You know! You see it!
You know exactly what's going on in here!
I don't want to swallow any more tears.
I've wasted much of my younger years
Running from this glass house.

Running?

Maybe.

I live in a glass house.
You can hear the cackles.
You can see my shackles.
You can see my tears,
In this house made of glass.

Trophy Children

People are coming to visit.
You start a pot of coffee and demand that we clean.
We dust the high shelves, they'll be here any minute.
This role you play will be your best scene.

There's no time for mistakes, so we comb our own hair.
Don't say a word unless someone speaks to you.
You get out the scrapbook and get yourself prepared.
Mother of the year, we've learned to pretend, too.

We're just your trophy children.
Only for show, like the pictures on your shelf,
Like portraits in a frame.
You only thought of yourself,
Only wanted to protect your own name.

You put on a great act for everyone.
But the light in your eye is from a shallow space,
For the door is shut and the game is done.
Your trophies never want to come back to this place.

Family Trip

Mommy and daddy won't stop fighting.
So that's why I'm in my room writing.
I swear to God, I'm used to the yelling.
Better keep my mouth shut, there's no telling.

Let's go on a vacation.
Maybe we need a family trip.

Can she see out of that black and swollen eye?
And damn that scar, she stabbed him with a knife.

Normal normal normal, let's pretend it's ordinary.
I scrub myself, but I still feel like a dirty baby.

I feel bugs crawl across my skin, but they're not there.
I dig deep into my skin, don't you care?
Feed us lies and poison, to kill our talents.
The medicine won't solve this chemical imbalance.

Trophy Children II

You want to show everyone that you're the best parent.
But when we're alone, I don't know where that went.

You make yourself a stranger when we leave the house.
My mouth is quiet because talking about it isn't allowed.

You see, you and I are different – so don't compare us.
You're the one who broke any part of me willing to trust.

I've lived through the clouds and the storms.
I made it out alive but not in the same form.

What if some things just stay broken,
And you can't fix them?

Hostage

You're holding me hostage, will I ever escape the woods?
I've planned my escape, but I don't know if I should.
What would happen to me if I were to get caught?
Would you find me, and would a lesson be taught?

This cage is shrinking
And making me more claustrophobic every day.
We arrive at the courthouse
And you give me a script to say.

Everything is fine.
It was all a huge misunderstanding, you see!

There's nothing wrong; no one is fucking tormenting me.

Interview

Tell me what's been happening.
I try to remember the words they had told me to say.

Hmm?
I shrug my shoulders, nervous that they'll take me away.

You know...
What you say here is going to stay between you and me.

I look up.

I confessed.

As if I was the one who'd committed the crime.

I Told the Truth

A confession is burning the inside of my soul.
Descriptions of characters in my heart take a toll.

I need a way to break free from these illusions.
I escape this dimension but might take a bruising.

I go to a beautiful island where I feel sublime.

I don't feel any fear anymore.

Not one bit.

Secret's out.

Trophy Life

No one was aware of the secrets you keep.
They still think your heart is made of gold.
And when it's mentioned, they find it hard to believe
The fear I get after school when I come home.

Because I'm told that you knew I told.
And telling is bad.

I didn't mean to ruin your perfect image, darling.
I'm so sorry that your show is ending.
But you still insist on pretending.
No! No?
No.

It's absurd, but you lie straight through your teeth.
I can't believe there still are people who
Think you are royalty.
That you're lovely.
No! No?
No.

Your trophies fell off the shelf.
They don't exist.
So, where's your reputation now?
What's your crutch? What's your vice?
Where do you run?
You have nothing now.
How does that feel?

Well, how does it feel?

Sirens

Sirens, sirens.
Coming from a distance.
It was late, it was dark,
But I saw flashing lights on top of the car.
It was bedtime, I was scared.
But where were you? You weren't there.
He had weapons ready for use.
You defended his honor in spite of the abuse.

I could only hear the sirens,
I could only see the lights.
It's like nothing else existed that night.
Everything changed, a new rock bottom.
Innocence preserved in a freezer, still fucking rotten.

I bet they caught you by surprise.
You should've seen the look in your eyes.
But it wasn't justified.
You were only charged with a DUI,
When you've done so much worse.

Police sirens, police sirens.
Painting my nightmares red and blue.
A reminder of everything I was about to lose.

Put us in the back of the car.
Drive us away now, really far.
Over the moon, over the rainbow.
There's more to life than what we know.

The Rescue

We are rescued.
We are starting over.
But what does that mean?

New horizons, new town, new people.
New world, new life.
I'm in a place where no one knows my name.

Teacher asks me to say a fun fact about myself.

I shrug.

I've lost myself in the toxic house I just left.

But we'd been freed to a good life, a better life.

At least, that's what we thought.

Who She Was.../...Who She Is

She cooked dinner before, now we fend for ourselves.
She had cable installed, but he cut the cords with scissors.
Her eyes were emerald green.
Now they were black.
Swollen shut.

She was a good mother before, so I was told.
Now she is merely a corpse, dead beauty walking.

She built a paradise behind four walls,
And he infiltrated our home.
She used to walk so proudly with her head up.
But now she stares down, dodging landmines.

She told her daughter to run away,
Because she couldn't go herself.
Then she got angry and felt abandoned.
She threw guilt, but she was not innocent.

But what if we are all to blame? she asked.

I shake my head.

Nothing could be more wrong.

None of us knew how to deal with the situation.
True, very true.
There is no manual.

Family separated and moved thirty-five miles south,

A foreign place with no one familiar.
Feeling disrupted and out of our skin; caught in between.

Grade school classmates wondered where we came from
And why we moved.
I wasn't sure how to answer them.

As my new teacher lectured about George Washington,
I remembered I had left my favorite shirt back north.
I wondered if it was donated,
Or still in the back of my closet.

The sheets on my new bed
Were not clean and did not smell fresh.

Where were mine?
The blue ones with the stars and stripes on them?

I guessed they were packed away.

Like my old toys
And the coloring books I did with mother.

Packed away with so much.

PART TWO
the unraveling

Dwell

Mother said to me, *you can't dwell on the past,*
And I know that's true.
But that doesn't mean forgiveness
Should be rewarded to you.
You don't know what it's like
To wake up screaming in the night.

I really had only one option left here,
And I'm sorry if this leads my sister to tears.
Red rivers escaping my veins leave me less confused.
It makes it possible to face the battles I've yet to lose.

There are times I wake up happy to be alive.
But then there are days when I struggle just to get by.
I think to myself, *why can't I feel good every day?*
Why does this cycle repeat and always be the same?

I'm not dwelling on the past.
It's just not written in a self-help book
Explaining just how long it takes
Until I'm magically cured.

Some people change,
And some don't want to.
I expect nothing from you.
Dwell on that.

Before You Came Along

If only I could be the person I was before
My mother brought you through the door.
Before your fists were your version of a hug.
She said your kiss was like a drug.

Too bad she couldn't overdose on him.

Who?

I heard my coworkers discussing
Who they would bring back to life
For one night.

I thought to myself, *my aunt and my uncle.*

They lived next door when I was at my mother's.
They were inspirations of what love should be like.

But when my aunt passed on,
My uncle became a ghost on earth.
Sold the house
And other people took it over.

It was an invasion.
I wasn't welcome there unannounced—
In the house where I used to spend sweet nights.

Invasion

Who are these invading strangers?
They're bringing in furniture in big trucks.
We thought you had more time.
But even with prayers there wasn't any luck.

There are still some of your clothes in boxes.
These new homeowners placed them on the stoop.
I remember watching soap operas on your TV.
And I still have our last conversation on loop.

Months pass and I see the inside start to decay.
They're not taking good care of paradise lost.
It reeks with sewage, and fleas bite their legs.
Now you couldn't sell the house at half the cost.

You might as well have set fire to the old building.
The garage collapsed after we left in November.
The snow melted, but the memories remain.
Even after all these years, I still remember.

Yes, I have lost others.
But you were the first punch.
The house has been demolished.
And I had never felt so much.

A few months ago, construction started.
I still ride by so I can take a glance.
I wonder what you would think if you saw,
And how life would've been if we still had a chance.

I still recall dirt clumps, carpets,
The smell of chocolate milk.
How I preferred uncle's because it was sweeter than yours.
Scented markers, fresh coffee, and smooth silk.

You measured our heights on the wall,
Labeled our ages, the date, and the time.
Although I am older now and create new memories,
Those were the days when I felt most alive.

You're still here. And that home is still yours.
I still see you playing basketball.
Too old to be that active;
I didn't know it then.

I'll always remember,
Even as I stare at the new walls.

It doesn't look as good as it used to.

First Loss

I was only seven years old when they took you away.
It was the first time in my life that I felt true pain.
I didn't know what I was supposed to say.
I woke up the next morning thinking you'd be there,
And that maybe you would take us to the Boonville Fair.

If You Were Still Alive Today

It's been so long since I've seen you.
Thinking about it makes me want to cry.
Tell me, why did you have to go?
And dance with rusty-haloed angels?
I never saw it coming.
I had twenty missed calls one morning.

I've got a question for you.
But being rejected is such a huge fear.
If you were still alive today...
Would you look at me and turn away?
Would you hate who I am?
Or would you understand?

If you were still alive today...
Would you still love me like you did
Back when I was just a kid?

Another moment with you is all I wish.
Just one more familiar wet kiss.
I never thought things would turn out like this.
I never thought you would have to be missed.
You were the first goodbye to start my list.

If You Were Still Alive Today II

If you were still alive today...
Would you love me for me?
Be what I need?
Hug me like you used to?
I want to play Mario with you again.

If you were still alive with us now,
I would cherish you.
Ask you to read me Green Eggs and Ham.
Listen to you sing Patsy Cline.
And hope you'd give me another bear, to be all mine.

Ongoing Thoughts

Sometimes there are too many thoughts that eat me away.
I beg for mercy, but until the night is through, they stay.
It's exhausting to put on a brave face for the world.
I'm told to *man up and stop whining like a little girl.*
But my mind can keep me chained.

Some days are good, as if I'm pure and clean.
But there are moments when I'm desperate to break free.
It's an ongoing battle, even as I write these words.
I can go from peace to despair in one moment;
I never know when it'll occur.

I've read about challenging anxiety head first.
Sometimes it helps, but sometimes it's much worse.
Is that all you got? Come on anxiety, give me more!
Sometimes it deepens my mental war.

Sometimes I want to be normal
For just one day.

The Sun

The sun doesn't come out much anymore.
I have come back full circle.
I swore I would do better this time.
All I want is to feel fine.
This life means so much to me.
Please set this pain free.

I do.

As I bleed.

Different

Court ordered visitation trips, guilt trips.
More lies continuously leaving her lips.
Things will be different if you come home.

My siblings and I already know...
But all three of us return in one way or another.
We were manipulated.
Me, my sister, and my brother.
Home...sweet...home.

Things will be different, she said.

The Quiet Game

This heavy rope can't get much tighter.
I get exhausted from being a fighter.
Bursting my arteries and my shiny veins,
With a sharp razor and self-inflicted pain.
This was a lie of a life I didn't ask for.

Starving myself for the bitter taste of perfection.
Cracking the mirror when I look at my reflection.
I hear the monsters whisper my name.
They make me play the quiet game.
Can't tell, won't tell, don't tell.
Or things won't turn out well.

I remember more every day.
God, make these feelings go the fuck away!
The monsters will not be tamed,
So let's play the quiet game.
Shh….

Free Promo

There's a lot of guilt.
There's a lot of shame in what I do.
I'm not proud of it.
I'm not promoting it.
I'm not saying that it's okay,
And I know there is help.
There are resources out there.
However, my parents don't want me to get better.
They want to hurt me.
They want to torture me.
There has to be a way out, though…

Scriptures

Scriptures, plastered all over my body.
I just don't want to be a nobody.
Trying to get a second of attention
Was always too much to mention,
To ask for.

I just want to matter.
Not shatter.

My heart has been discarded,
I'm told I'm retarded.
Became a spade.
But this is how I was made.

Blood relative,
But didn't know it was bad blood.

My home is in the dirt,
And dinner is mud.

Under Long Sleeves

Hiding the truth under long sleeves.
It's true that love only leaves.
You get attached and hope for the best.
Learning that everyone is just like the rest.
I feel like I deserve to be treated this way.
It's no surprise that no one stays.

Is it normal to feel like this?
Is it okay to be okay with it?

I have to go back to class now
And figure out how to stop the bleeding somehow.
The stinging, a sensation—a relief.

Well?

Why didn't you ever ask how I felt
About the cards that we were dealt?

Evil Man

What's a home? What's a home?
All my life, I've only been alone.
A prisoner in my own skin,
Truly afraid of my protector.
Mirages are frequent in my life.
Illusions delight my eyes...
Which I then open, so tired, to screams,
Having to leave my perfect dreams.

My self-esteem quickly vanishes.
Happiness is banished.
With glasses breaking,
I was mistaken
To think the earth was quaking.
It was the evil man again.
It was the evil man once again.

Content

I can't remember
What it's like
To feel content.

I need some serotonin
For my brain
To be sent.

Friendly Competition

I say that I'm sad, you say that you're sad.
I say that I'm hurt, you say that you're hurt.
I bleed down my scarred wrist.
Like thin lines on paper showing a list.
You then lock yourself in the bathroom
And pick at your skin with a razor, too.

Is this a friendly competition we are having here?
Are you on the brink too, my dear?
You can't go a second without someone
Acknowledging only your pain.
Like you're the only one allowed
To struggle day by day.

Sorry to take the attention away from you.
But I'm going through some shit, too.
And I don't want to see who can hurt themselves more.
Because I don't want to hurt anymore.

Shock

Shock, shock. Shock, shock.

I feel the energy running through me.
This is more awakening than coffee.
Shock!

You made a choice and took it all away from me.
All that's left here is my discarded dignity.
You've disappeared and I have nothing to eat.
I swallow a rotten fruit and it's still sweet.

Today, I decided to take a bubble bath with a hair dryer.
I was told that I'm handsome but such an ugly crier.
Shock!

I consume sweet poison like it's some sort of contest.
I drown out the demons because I'm so fucking depressed.
I ignore the memories that I work hard to suppress.
The truth serum is getting hard to process.

My body is an empty casket, but not as pricey.
All this time, I feel something is missing in me.
Shock!

I told the doctors that something just doesn't feel right.
There are monsters and they come out late at night.
They said *talk to your parents, they're all you have.*
I said—*are you crazy? They'll just laugh!*

I try to make connections with people

Who don't give a fuck.
Connect the cord into the outlet and I get some bad luck.
Oh, no!
Who knew there would be a storm coming about?
Before I could throw the hairdryer in, the power went out.

I dunk myself under and I can still hear thunder...

Splash.

Water

The water is rising, and it's over my head.
I count backwards and hum until I'm dead.
I wiggle my toes and drift along with the waves.
I hope no one notices and tries to get me saved.

I've waited for an accident to happen for far too long.
Can't tie a noose or take pills because I'm not that strong.
Strength to give up, strength to find peace.

But I come up for air,
Because…

It's not my time to leave

yet.

Bathroom Break

I excuse myself to the boy's bathroom.
I hide my weapon of choice in my sock.
A shiny razor.
I kiss it softly.
Then I sing a song in my scattered head.
Now I can breathe again.
My dirty little secret.

Mindfulness

I'm losing my mind.   I'm losing my mind.

I'm losing my mind.   I'm losing it.

I'm losing it.

Doing things I can't remember.

Doing things to numb the pain.

I'm losing my mind.   I'm losing my mind.

I'm losing my mind.   I'm losing it.

I feel like I'm about to crack.

Wasn't Me

Whoever did that wasn't me.
I'm sorry, you must have made a mistake.
I was just sipping on a green tea.
Surely, that monster doesn't have my face.

Hey, didn't you hear me?
Aren't you listening here?
Hello? It wasn't me. I said it wasn't me!
So don't expect me to feel guilty.
Maybe it was a body double? I don't know.
You need to let the conspiracy go.
Whoever did that wasn't me.

What? You don't think I have the decency
To own up to my own faults? Well…
Hmm...well, I hope you rot in hell!
Matter of fact, how about I send you there.
Bang, bang, and all the people stare.

Wow! Pull it together!
God, who am I becoming?
Shh! Don't let them know the feelings you're feeling.

I act like I witnessed a crime.
But I'm not going to say it was me this time.
It wasn't me. Nope!
Maybe it was him.
He looks suspicious!
Why are you looking at me?
Are you finished?

Oh...wait.

Is it because I laugh like a maniac and eat lunch alone?
Dig into my skin with a razor at half past one?
Hide in the bathroom and watch the blood drip?
In the flood from my vein, I hope no one slips.
But that wasn't me either!
None of that was me.
You think I'm crazy?

That wasn't me!

I'm not guilty!

Send Help

I'm unraveling.
　　I'm unraveling.
　　　　I'm unraveling.
　　　　　　I'm unraveling.
　　　　　　　I'm unraveling.
　　　　　　I'm unraveling.
　　　　　I'm unraveling.
　　　　I'm unraveling.
　　　I'm unraveling.

Time for Truth

We need to talk to you, they say.

I look up.

I remember speaking with people dressed like that before.
When I was caught doing what I was doing.
I told them I was fine, that I had stopped.

Uh...oh...

Enabling Habits

My crippled heart seeks a bright light.
Living on the outside scares me at night.
I'm a slave to this family.
They just want to hurt me.

Sharp razors cut into my flesh.
How can I be optimistic when hope has left?

I declare war on myself.
The target is the man in the mirror staring back.
I feel like there's no help for me.

Another Secret Is Out

Uh, oh.

Secret's out.

You caught me.
I told you I had stopped.

Secret's out.

You know about it.
Lock me away?

Fine.
That's fine.
At least I'll be away from you…

PART THREE
the Titanic's foundation

Sirens II

Wee woo, wee woo.

Sirens, ringing in my ears.
Sirens, reminding me of my fears.

I should've been afraid of snakes.
But I was scared to be awake,
Making a sound that caused a floor creak.
And now as I grow, I still feel so weak.
Even today, I can still hear her screams.
They haunt me now, even in my dreams.

I work at a coffee shop now.
I see police officers come in and smile.
It makes me nervous.
Small reminders send me back to when I was a child.
Getting ready for bed, having school the next morning.
School, the only retreat from my home.
My own hell.

Sirens, sirens.
Flashing lights.
Sirens, so deafening.
I was ten years old at the time.
Sirens, so taunting.
I made a song out of it.

Wee woo, wee woo.
Wee woo, wee woo.

I still remember riding in the back of an ambulance.
Arriving at my destination so slowly,
Yet, so fast if that makes sense.

Sirens, coming from a distance.
Take me away to what I've been missing.

Wee woo.

In a Gown

I woke up and I was wearing a hospital gown.
And then I was in an ambulance heading across town.
What's going on? Where am I going?
And why, for the first time in my life,
Do I want my parents by my side?

Confusion

What is this place they have forced me into?
It looks like a school, it feels like a prison.

People just like me.
We sit in a circle and share how we feel.

I feel confused.

Confused because I thought I was the only one who felt…
Worthless, hopeless, constantly depressed.
Anxious, discarded, like nothing made sense.

Are you telling me that other people feel this way?
Is that supposed to bring me comfort?
No one should feel like this.

But it's not my turn to speak.

Inpatient Care

Inpatient therapy.
Let's heal this poor child.
His behavior is much too wild.
Your parents care, they really do.
They have unconditional love for you.
They're here to visit, let's guide you to the room.
I can still smell my mother's perfume,
And she blames it all on me.
But I'll heal here, I believe.
I'll be away from the people who have scarred me
Much worse than I've done to myself.

Impatient Care

You care that I get the care that I need.
How come I didn't get that from my family?
I'm not insane,
I've just gone crazy
From all the shit I've seen.

Safe from Harm

The doctors think they have it all figured out.
Shattered glass, flecked into my arms.
They said they'd keep me safe from harm.
Then why will they send me home afterwards?

Why Do That?

Why hurt yourself? they ask me.
It was to set my pain free.
I had no choice. It became a bad habit.
Like smoking cigarettes.
I could breathe again every time I held my blade.
It was me taking on the world with a clean slate.
I did it so much, I couldn't stop giving into the impulse.
I both feared and expected for the loss of my pulse.

I didn't want to die, but I didn't care if I did.
I didn't think anyone would miss the *useless kid*.
I didn't hurt myself to try to put an end to it, though.
It was more me holding onto life than letting go.
Just push on a little longer, until you're eighteen.
And then when you get the chance, you can run free.
Free from your family. Free from the abuse.
My weapon of choice was a very good use.

Group

We've been to rock bottom.
Pushed on when we didn't want to.
Felt afraid in our own homes,
Surrounded but still feeling alone.
Now we're all connected.
I don't know how to accept this.
Saying goodbye, my eyes will well up as we exit.

I will never forget you.
Any of you.
You know who you are.
You made me realize that I'm not alone in this world.

Show Me Your Scars

Have you ever been emotionally naked before?
Have you ever just laid it all out on the line?
Do you not see what's worth fighting for?
Show me your scars, and I'll show you mine.
Show me your scars, and it'll be fine.

I will be your lighthouse, your guiding hope.
I will show you love, I will give you scope.
Open your eyes, don't see this as weakness.
You can move mountains, and you will shine.
Just show me your scars, and I'll show you mine.

Men and Mental Illness

There are other males here in this ward.
It's still crazy to think because…
I've heard it so many times before.

Man up! Grow a pair! Stop acting like a little girl!
Boys don't cry! Don't be such a pussy!
Well...go ahead. Shrink me. Make my problems not real.
Boys are supposed to be tough!
You're such a sissy.

Why do I hear this often when guys talk about issues?
It's hard enough to talk about these problems as it is.
For no one to take it seriously,
To brush it off.
It's a shame.

I have a messed-up mind.
That doesn't make me less of a person.
Less of a man.
Why's that so hard to understand?

Fellow Diagnosis

I hold your hand and say,
you shouldn't have been through the shit you have.
And I know sometimes that you feel
Like you don't have an arm to grab
And no one to talk to.
But that's not true.
Don't tie the noose.
The world needs more people like you.

I'm Speaking Now

Scars all over my body.
I wanted to talk to somebody.
But no one would pay attention.
Even when it was necessary to mention.
It's not all fun and games now, is it?
Denying parent's visits, so easy to resist it.

I hope you regret this.
Because I've met many amazing people on this journey.
So I'm going to remember what they've given me,
And what they have taken away.

I refuse to be the tyrants that they are.

Circle

I didn't think I'd come to this place.
Seeing you all, standing face to face.
And in this circle, full of comfort inside.
I finally have no reason to hide.

We share stories of traumas past.
How the pain in our hearts seems to last.
And in this circle, full of love inside,
I have no reason to hide.

Happy

I'm so glad I came here.
I'm so glad I punched a mirror.
And as cheesy as it would seem,
You have all truly saved me.
I've never felt so accepted.
All my life, I've been rejected.

I thought you would all hate me,
But now we've become a family.
And for once, I can say I am happy.
Or at least I want to be.

Who Am I?

Sometimes I feel like a new person every four days.
A different perspective and mindset in every way.
I feel in tune with the world, redefined.
A brand new chapter that's all mine.
The sky is a different shade of blue.
And again, suddenly I feel brand new.
Fresh options, like a squeezed grapefruit.
I have a new identity and a different route.

Some may say this is growth, this is great.
But then why does it make me so damn afraid?
I have to stop and think…

Wait.
Who am I?

What makes me like this?
Was it because I grew up without parents?
Putting my own needs on hold.
Believing every cruel word told.
I used to think I was beyond bold–
But that was a week ago.

Dignity

Don't you know that your smile makes my day?
I'm going to cry when we have to go our separate ways.
I felt the rains pouring down on me.
I just wanted my pain to escape and leave.
You looked at my wrists and said, *have some dignity.*

Love Away

Note to self:

You give your love away to people who don't deserve it.
You look for approval that you never will get.
After everything that happened to you
When you were a kid,
You just want someone to make you feel alive.
But you're only hurting yourself in the meantime.
I know you're just trying to get by,

But you break your own heart more every day.
You wear yourself out by blindly giving love away.
You are more than enough, and you will be loved.

Hurts Most

I see new patients come into this psych ward.
Every single one that passes looks so lost.
I want to reach out and hug them all.
I wish there was something that I could do.
No one should have to feel so hurt.

Will you please just smile? It's tearing me apart.
I wish I could fix your wounded heart.

But I can't.
I can't.

And that's what hurts the most.

So Much

Sometimes I feel like I'm my own best friend.
I'll be there for myself until the end.
But I also feel like my own worst enemy.
I'm the one who is constantly bullying me,
Reminding myself of all my failures.
I realize now those are a blur.

I have accomplished so much.

Survived so much.

Fought for so much.

I am so much.

Counting

Day one and counting...
Finally, a chance to be heard.
Or a chance for tears to burst.
But it wouldn't be the first.
Because my life has been far worse.

Day two and counting...
I feel like I belong.
Like I found a reason to be strong.
That nothing I could do would be wrong.
I wonder if I'll be in this asylum for long.

Day three and counting...
Tensions start to rise.
Knowing we will one day say goodbye.
We've all become so close, and I
Finally feel so identified.

Day four and counting...
Days are slowly slowing.
I can't continue without knowing
That soon we'll be going.
After all our scars we've been showing.

Day five and counting...
Can't say that we didn't see this coming.
Still the aftertaste is a bit stunning.
Our only solution was running.
There is more to life incoming.

Day eight and counting...
There were moments I wish I could wish away.
But there was a message today.
Cherish every moment while you can stay.
But there will be times you'll drown by rain.

Day nine and counting…
Just when I thought I could be happy
I realize that love only leaves.
Why? This can't really happen in true serenity.
Is this how it's supposed to be?
I hope you won't forget me.

Day eleven and counting…
Like a bullet in my chest.
I haven't stopped crying since you left.
You are not like the rest.

Day thirteen and counting...
A fever comes so fast.
Tell me how much longer this pain will last?

The final day and counting…
It's now or never.
Feels like I been here forever.
Me and my home...we need to be together.

Sleep Well

Sleep well…
Close your eyes.

I can't say that I didn't see it coming,
But I never expected it to happen so soon.
Honestly, I was just running and running.
I didn't ever want to face the truth.
If we don't leave this place, we'll never make a better life.
So unfortunately, this is our final last good night.

You better sleep well, darling.
I don't think I'll be getting any rest.

How am I supposed to be sleeping
When all I can think about is your leaving?
If you don't leave, you'll never make it far.
I want you to know, I love you for all that you are.

Farewell

I'm going home.
This road made of dirt
Has memories, full of hurt.
Some I regret,
And some I'd love to forget.

Teachers

Teachers are glancing over at me when I return to school.
They whisper. And do the fake smile thing.
They know about what's happened.
And why I've been absent.

I sink into my seat further.

Something I Wish I Knew Back Then

You can get all the help you want.
Get therapy, get medication.
But if you're still around your triggers…
You will never be free.

As for myself, after I left the mental hospital,
I could only do so much while still in my parent's care.

But I left them and my past behind a couple years later.
That's when true freedom was born,
And I learned what real life was like.

PART FOUR
the highs and lows

The Worst Part

Every day is a new ***the worst part...***
The worst part of living with the metal disorders that I or anyone has.

The worst part is not knowing if the relationships failed because of incompatibility or because of how you are.

Not knowing if you're getting any better or if the medication is working,
Or maybe you're just having a bad day and that's why things are going awry.

Maybe you're just having a bad reaction to the new medicine being prescribed.

The worst part is having wonderful days and then having a bad day and feeling like it's going to never end.
Being so high on life one day and the next feeling so low that you're finding a home in the dirt.

The worst part is not knowing how long you've been lost or have felt this way.
Not knowing how to respond when people say *tell me about yourself.*

What's true and what's not?
Who am I without the disorder I carry every day?
My identity?
Who? Who? Who?

I can't keep blaming everything on my fucked-up childhood.
I have to take some responsibility.
There comes a point where it's my choice.

The worst part is feeling so in control of your life but then losing the momentum and drive to keep that concept going.

The worst part is feeling so defensive when someone looks at me.

The worst part is flinching when someone makes a sudden movement towards me.

The worst part is that not many people take this shit seriously.
They don't see this as a real illness, but in my darkest hours I feel like my mind is rotting.

I want to dig my nails into my body and release myself—a person who has to hide because it's not socially acceptable to talk about the fact that at work there are moments when I want to walk into the freezer and scream at the top of my lungs.

Too often I hear…
I get so anxious before a test!
I am sooooo OCD about this!
And wow! My mom is sooooo bipolar!

They don't even know what it's actually like.

The worst part is feeling like I'll drive people away when I open up about the truth.

The worst part is feeling like everyone will leave.
That there's a new crisis every day.

Feeling like I disappoint the ones that I love.

Going through a point in my life when I looked at
someone I admired and asked *why can't I love you when
I'm sober?*

The worst part is that people get sad when someone
commits suicide but when someone shows symptoms of
depression they are told that they are only looking for
attention.

I never really understood the whole looking for attention
thing because **everybody** wants attention. Everyone wants
to be noticed. To be acknowledged.

Every day is a new the worst part.

Angry

Angry, frustrated. I'm mad as hell.
I can't remember the last time I felt something other than anger.
I'm burdened with the explanation to why I keep you a stranger.

Angry, frustrated! Wow! I'm angry!

I am angry because of what I have I missed out on.
I am angry because all I was ever told was that I was wrong.
I am pissed the fuck off because I feel guilty when I smile.
I am angry since my so-called recovery is taking a while.

Angry, frustrated! Wow! I'm mad!
I am furious because you refuse to own up to what you've done.
I am furious because I have to apologize for all the tar in my lungs.
I am furious because I'm sick of using the excuse of **you** for why I am so messed the hell up!

Angry! Angry! Damn it!

I'm angry because I am so defensive.
I'm angry because I am too sensitive.
I am angry because I am! I am because I am angry!
And I'm angry because I'm confused.

I am confused about why it had to be me.

I am confused with how to connect with my identity.
I am confused because I can't understand basic skills.
I am confused and afraid that I always will be.

I am angry because I want to ask my sister about her side
of the story, but I don't have the courage for that.

I am angry because even when people show they care,
I feel like they're against me and I push them out like I
always do.

I am angry because my family is broken, and I can't pick
up the phone to ask my brother about my niece and
nephew.

I am angry because I just want to make peace with these
stitches I have.

Don't get me wrong,
I'm grateful to be alive.
I want the people I love to know they made a crazy
impact.

But sometimes I want to scream and break the sound
barrier, with you holding my hand.
Thank you for sticking this out with me, even though it
can be hard to understand.

Elixir

Do you know what it's like to be dirty?
To have rattlesnakes grab at your throat?
To have these sad vices as your scapegoat?
There is a new seed, planted within my veins.
Stitch it up, harvest the root without any shame.
Wake up and feel the decay, I rot.
Suddenly, you connect the dots.
How I boil to the surface, climb the tower.
I have the true elixir.
Gulp. Puff. Cough. Slurp.

Anything not to feel.
So desperate not to.

Desperation

I used to cling to relationships with all my might.
The presence of a lover helped me through the night,
Gave me some hint of the love that I never had from my
parents.

I was desperate and begging...
Not wanting to be thrown out...
But often they got sick of me.
They had enough of the sadness, enough of charity.

I would quickly find someone new
To fill the hole in my heart.
It helped.

And when they left too,
I desperately clutched onto someone else.
And the cycle would head back to the start.

I just needed to feel loved by someone.
Anyone.
I was so desperate.

Anxiety Attack

Let it begin--the nail biting, the pacing, and overthinking.
Looking over my shoulder, fearing the worst will happen.
Feeling exhausted by trying to make eye contact.
How do I get over this? How do I feel normal?
Does anyone have a manual?
I'll take thirty copies and I'll treat them like my bible.
Because I'm getting tired of writing these poems.
Can't I write about struggles that aren't within this realm?
The catacomb within myself.
The iceberg frozen, I will it to melt –
Is there a way my cold heart can be no more?

What's the meaning of this?
How is it so easy for some people?
Maybe we have our own battles, yeah.
We all must have our own battles, but this one's mine.

Breathe in, Breathe Out

I thought I would be better by now.
I thought I would've turned it around somehow.
But here I am, trying to understand.
Why is it that I'm still struggling on the same path?
Only hanging by a little thread?

All I am familiar with are these walls,
Knuckle shaped holes covering them.
People acted like I was lying,
That it was the furthest thing from the truth.
That's why there was no use in trying.
How could the monster you are really be you?

I know I have to go on.
I know I have to breathe in, breathe out.
I have to see what this life has to offer.
Because I do deserve that.
I do deserve that.

Why?

But it's just so hard.
One day I can be on top of the world.
The next day I can be at rock bottom again.
Who knew recovery would be this hard?

What am I even recovering from?
Why can't it be easier?
Why can't my mind function normally?
Why?

Strive

I was always a unique child,
Always had my own way of doing things.
I didn't know my way of thinking was truly unsettling.
Do you want to be my distraction for the time being?
Help get my mind off the crazy shit I've been seeing?
I'm not afraid of clowns, ghosts or ghouls.
I was simply terrified of coming home from school.

I've tried. I've tried. I've tried.
I swear I've tried but I can't fix what she's broken.
I've died. I've died. I've died.
I can't fix what she has shattered to bits.
And I can't be involved in her dramatic skits.

Imagine me as a kid, smiling wide while I say,
Nobody listens to me, so I crisscross my veins every day.
I have eight cavities in my teeth and fresh tears.
I'm fourteen years old and I want to disappear.

She had a garden and she grew dead crops.
She couldn't slow down, she couldn't stop.

I've tried. I've died. I've lied and I strive.
I fight. I ignite. I thrive and again I strive.
I can't unfreeze her frostbitten core.
I have no use for her anymore.

Distraction

You are just a distraction.
Something I can use to my advantage.
What's in it for me?
I need a way out of my head.
Maybe I'll lose these demons in your bed.
I'll transfer them as we exchange spit.
Please tell me that you'll bear it.

You're another distraction, just like this drink.
It's a way to shake it off, so I don't think.
Why would I want to focus on what's real?
That means actually dealing with how I feel.
No, thanks! That's not what I need.
I'll just allow my mind to be foggy.

I've spent a long time living this way.
Dead man walking, numbing away the shame.
They say I just need to get out to the city.
The reaper will be gone and I will be free.
I feel so feral. I feel absorbed in isolation.

You and these distractions help me escape.
If I lose touch, I know I can refrain,
Because I'm the one who has control here.
Don't flatter yourself; I'll hurt you, dear.
I am in a dark place, and I want a way out.

So go on and distract me.
Be my distraction of the week.
Until you get sick of having to deal with my brain.

Distract me. Get me out of this pain.
So go on, distract me. It's all I know.
Make me forget, make it go.

Forgot About Me by Now

You probably forgot about me by now,
And honestly, I'm not surprised.
Even though you looked me in the eyes,
Tears fell from yours, and it wasn't like before.
This can't be happening.

How am I supposed to keep my head held up high?
The last time you saw me you said,
You know this isn't goodbye.
But now I see that you don't remember me.
It's been so long since we spoke.

I watch your car drive down the end of my street.
When I can't see you anymore is when I believe
You never really cared.

I went back to my old habits,
Because I couldn't deal with this.
Begged... God! I can't believe I begged you.
That's something the me now would never do.
I was at my lowest low and had no dignity.
Obsessed with filling the hole in me with codependency.

You don't know what it's like to need a way out so much
That you will do anything or anyone,
Not thinking about the holes in your heart.
A cloudy mind, living in a daze.
You probably forgot about me,
But I remember you until this day.

I cried out and an echo shook the earth.
I still remember sirens, the back of the ambulance.
Where were you? I haven't heard from you since.
Have I even crossed your mind?
I guess I never meant to you as much as you meant to me.

You probably forgot about me by now.
You forgot me, didn't you?
Yeah, I believe that.
You probably forgot about me by now, honey.
Right?

The Replacements

Is this what we as humans do?
Go on with life trying to replace the people we miss most?
I found a certain safety with someone else.
The person reminds me of you, you know.
You're so different, but the connection I feel is the same.

Drink to Get Drunk

I drink the bottle down until there's nothing left.
I lift the bottle up, let it drip so I have every drop I can get.
I drink to get drunk.

I have become a regular at the local liquor store.
The owner knows me because they've seen me before.
They placed my order because I've sold them out.
I bought every sample left in the house.

I drink to get drunk, just to feel numb,
To feel like someone.
I can fly, I can fly.
No pain inside.

Growth

I've watched myself in photos, watched myself grow.
But what really is growth? I want to know.
My heart pines for a life.
Something out of my reach.
Something not like what I have seen.
The future delivers it to me on a silver platter.
For once, I realize that I do matter.

Sober in the Clouds

I didn't know how to love you when I was sober.
And I didn't know how to love myself when I was sober.
Equations can't be explained.
I feel so freaking drained, depleted.
Weakened, tired of competing,
Fighting a battle that I'm not sure can be won.
Filling up my lungs, with smoke.

I crash down and I realize that all that I have
And all that I've lost that was never really mine.
All that I strive for is to make up for time.
Lost time that sends chills up my spine.
I'm never getting those years back.

Wanting to move on from the mistakes I made,
And to learn simple things
That I should've learned as a kid,
Trying to understand social skills,
But my parents only wanted a thrill.
Now I struggle for the will
To find courage, to enjoy life,
Without following in their footsteps.

Sometimes I feel like every week I'm a whole new person,
And I have another life-altering revelation,
Thinking it's not a battle I can lose.

I feel like I evolve,
But then sometimes I am unaware of the habits I do,
My treatment of others and dangers I pursue.

After a while, you get accustomed to being used.

All my life I just shut my mouth, took a beating.
I said *all right, that's fine, you win, I'm defeated.*
People said *I love you,* but I felt like they didn't mean it.

As years went by, I guess I grew strong.
Fought back and at last I think of myself.
Yes! I want to be selfish. Call it what you want.
Selfishness, sure! I've been called much worse.
Say that I'm conceited.
I care about myself for the first time.

I never put myself first.
I was always last place.
Putting other people on a pedestal, with haste.
Thinking I was nothing but a waste.
Live life in a foggy haze, for days on end.
Time to hit the clouds yet again.

Being up in the clouds helped me transform.
At one time it did make me glad that I was born.
Fill the pipe, high as a kite.
Now things seem to be all right.
But still, something is missing within me.
Compromise myself and lose my dignity.
Looking for quarters in between the couch cushions.
I had no choice, it's what kept me pushing.
I wanted to forget so I could just live.
I did a good job. Yes, I did.

The Jungle

I remember running through the jungle.
Forty-five minutes across town to get to the train station
every day.
I carried my notebook and sat down on the dirty
pavement.
I would hear rumbling and I swear I could feel the ground
start to shake.

I don't know why I kept glancing up,
thinking you would get off the train and come running into
my arms.

I've waited for you.
I've been waiting here for you just in case you might want
to come back.

I've been here for hours.

I still have a glimmer of hope every time passengers exit
the train.
I remember once you said to meet you here and I searched
for you.

I turned around.
I caught you trying to surprise me.

But I found it hard not to notice you – I can sense your
energy miles away.
I can feel your aura... like a ghost taking over my body,
like a demon clinging to me.

I kept hoping you would change your mind,
and realize that I had nothing else at that time in my life.

You were everything.
I've lost so much that I didn't want to add to my list.

I waited there for you.

I ran through the jungle to the train station and paced
back-and-forth,
Saying to myself *any minute now...any minute now...*
You'll be here any minute now.
Because this was our secret place.
This was where it all began.

You spin me around like a vinyl.
Patterns, slow dancing, but the ride makes me queasy.
You think it's easy to love a lie?
To live on without recognizing the past is behind me?
Discarded dignity.

Sometimes I feel thrown out like spoiled food,
no good to you anymore.
Not worthy to taste your spit,
sweet and smooth,
like caramel and chocolate on a banana split,
ice cream so delicate and rich.

But you told me to ignore my fears.
Ignore the itch but it wasn't fair for me to pretend,
just like I always have before.
I deserve more and more and more.
I am not your carousel.
I am not capable of not getting dizzy.

I am not a compact disc.

I am not capable of starting from the beginning after the
ending draws close again.

I ran through the jungle.
I escaped the lions to get to the train station in which…

I would sit there hoping you would show up,
and it would be this amazing movie scene,
and we would live happily ever after.

Looking back, it was truly heartbreaking.
Desperate, lonely.
It was a jungle I was running through...
But I still ran for you.

Checking in

If I were at a store and you walked in, would you stop and smile?
Would we have a conversation?
I like to check in and see how you are every once in a while.
How are things with your family?

Nineteen

Truth is, even as time passes…
I am still reminded of the violent past.
Waking up to the screaming like it never ended.
I still had to endure it throughout my teens.
I was nineteen years old when I was able to break free.
All those years were filled with hell.
My parents were not healthy people.
They made me this anxiety, depressed, manic ridden
Person that I am now.

I'm still just trying to repair that.

PART FIVE
self-realization

Small Victories

They say you've got to celebrate the small victories.
Like looking someone in the eye,
Asking how their day is going.

They say you've got to celebrate the small victories.
Like being able to go through a day
Without having anxiety creep up my spine,
Hair raising goosebumps, a lump in my throat.
I can't figure out what's right or wrong.
My sense of reality isn't that strong.

But they say you've got to celebrate the small victories,
Like me...finally enjoying the holidays.
I do.

Merry Christmas.

Ideas

My therapist says...*hey, for every sad poem you write, you should try to write an optimistic one about what the future holds.*

And honestly, that's a great idea.

I Need

I need to give myself time to heal from what's happened.
I go through the phases, hoping it can make me feel better.
Cling to people and dream of a future together.
Desperation, craving for love somewhere.
Anywhere.

I need to give myself some time.
I need that.
I owe myself a chance.

I know what I need now.
I need to try to get better.
And I haven't tried.
Like really really tried,
but I will now.

I deserve a happy and long life.

Addiction

I am an addict. I've become addicted to hurting myself.
It was the only pain I could control.
It was to numb myself.
Physical pain hurt more than the emotional trauma
I was enduring.
I am addicted to hurting myself, but I'm sobering up.
I will be sober.

Addiction II

I am the fragrance,
I am the ghost viewing everything on the sidelines.
I'm an addict.
But I'm not the poor man living in the park,
Saving change to buy his bottle, savoring every last drop.
I do that at home, in my own bed,
And I'm doing fine financially.

I am addict. I have an addictive personality.
When I break one habit, I leech onto another.
A new schedule every week,
How will I escape the past this time?
Can't think about it, can't think.

I may be an addict,
But I'm not willing to mug or hurt anyone to get my fix.
I hurt myself enough, don't you see?
Like a snowball down a mountain.
The lies stretch wider and wider.

Addicts are everywhere.
They live relatively normal lives.
Doctors, counselors, policeman, teachers... yes, teachers…

The fifth grade teacher can't wait for the kids to go to
Recess so she can take a swig of bourbon.
They ask questions, she says she is tired.
She calls for silent reading.

Addicts aren't just one thing.

They aren't hookers selling away their body
On the corner of Third Street or Dudley Avenue.
They could get a decent paycheck
And have more than enough to spend,
Or they could ignore the phone calls from bill collectors,
Ignore the knocks on the door from rental centers,
Because they blew all their cash on a bag of snow.

Remembrance, permanence. Fragile.
It matters where you come from.
Sometimes I just feel so unfixable.
Sometimes I get so depressed that I wonder
How long I can hold my breath under my own bath water.
I want to be like one of the fish.
I want to be flying like a broken winged bird.

Sometimes battles seem meaningless.
Sometimes I feel like a joke.
That there's too much baggage when it comes to me.
I constantly feel the urge to apologize to my partner,
Because he ended up with someone like me – unidentified.

Not able to understand social cues,
Not able to notice the errors in my judgment.
I couldn't even make a phone call four years ago.
I couldn't speak.
I would walk with my head down,
Trying to remain unnoticed.
But I'm here. I'm here. God... I'm fucking here.
So take that, addiction!

Addiction can mean anything to anyone.
Anyone who is addicted to love or sex or coke or meth,
To cutting themselves to numb the pain
In a public restroom,
Or hiding vodka in their ginger ale bottle,

So when they walk down the street,
They just look parched.

Addiction is seen as this one idea,
This one thing,
And that's what society has done.
It's shameful.
So shameful.

Bad

Now, I'm not a bad person,
but I've done bad things before.
When I was broken, I hurt people I truly adored.

I was so blinded by a road to recovery that I lost
connections along the way.
I have shut people out when they kept trying and begging
to stay.

I can be cold as ice.
I can be as painful as a stab from a knife.
It gets overwhelming when you try to maintain control
over your life.

Now, I'm not a bad person,
but I've done bad things before.
Made others feel horrible to lift myself,
and I somehow loved myself more.

I have a past that I and no one else can change.
My background is a story filled with shame.

But haven't we all done fucked up shit?
Things we wish we could undo?
We've all done bad things, but we're not bad people.

Tired

I get so tired of listening to the same music,
watching the same movies, going to the same job.
I get so tired of seeing the same people,
walking the same town.
drinking the same tea,
dreaming the same dreams.
I get so tired of living the same lie,
drinking the same wine, having the same conversations.
making the same jokes and feeling the same pain.

I get so tired of using the same words,
thinking with the same mind,
waking up in the same bed,
loving the same people,
breathing the same air, writing the same poems,
eating the same food.
I get so tired of biting the same nails,
using the same vices,
causing the same trouble,
dealing with the same drama,
washing the same hair and repeating the same cycles.

I get so tired of making the same mistakes,
hearing the same myths,
feeling the same emotions,
crashing after the same high.

I get so tired of feeling.
Feeling feelings.
I get so tired of feeling everything.

Longing

Bright lights at the end of the tunnel.
That's what the TV says when babies are born.
But I wonder if my mother smiled at me
When she held me in her arms for the first time.
Or was she forlorn?
Longing for so much more...

Used to Be Fun

This used to be fun, self-medicating myself.
But now I realize that I might need some help.
This used to be fun, feeling untouchable, so high.
But it gets boring from doing it all the time.

I did it to distract myself from admitting the truth,
Repeating mistakes like my parents did in their youth.
How can I stop a problem when I don't know there is one?
What's the point in doing this? It used to be fun.
It used to be fun, but now I'm done.
This self-realization has me stunned.

I Am One of Them

You laugh, you make jokes.
I start to get a lump in my throat.
I silence myself, hush my voice.
You act as if this is a choice.

I hide myself in the dark.
I have too many scars,
And you have so much shit to say.
That's why I locked myself away.

Why is it so hard to understand?
I am one of them. I am one of those people,
That you constantly judge everyday.
You don't understand the shame;
That's why we keep our mouths shut.
No one to help us out of the rut.
Stop laughing. I am one of them,
And I can only do what I can.

There are too many reasons why.
You bring it up and I have to lie.
I try not to let it bother me,
But my heart fills up with anxiety.
I had a troubled childhood.
If I could act different then I would.
Ignorance will get you nowhere, no.
Learn something, so I can let this go.

You have so much shit to say,
That's why I lie every single day.

I only do what I can.
I am one of them, don't you understand?
I am just trying to be a man.
I am one of them, don't you understand?
I only do what I can.
I only do what I can.

Defensive

Why am I so defensive?
Why do I push away any company?
Why am I so protective?
Thinking everyone's out to get me?
You can look me in the eye and say you genuinely care.
I'll shrug it off and as if it's like I didn't hear you.
Instead I create false images,
Monsters so that I can fear you.
More monsters that follow me around like a shadow.
It's been like that since I was a kid, and I can't let it go.
It's all that I've known.

It has to stop.

I Wish

I wish I could enjoy being around people like others do.
But anxiety engulfs me like a cloud.
I'm standing there, but I'm not feeling very present.
I'm envious of people that can do it easily.
I have resentment. I'm jealous.
I wish that could be me.
Maybe one day it can be.

Only Human

I have an organic, trade-certified mindful free spirit.
Crazy conspiracies, does anyone want to hear it?
Sometimes humans have absolutely no humanity.
They hang people like slaves and not feel guilty,
but I will hug a stranger who cries in the corner.
Because I, too, have been pushed to the border.
I am identified, I am a man with a dream.
Rescue all the animals, they're sweet and cuddly.

I am only human. I am, I am.
I am only human. I am, I am.
I am on my way.

Life is a zoo,
but at least I can ride a fucking giraffe home.

The Blame Game/Eyes Are Open

How long have I felt like this?
How long have I been like this?
And how long will I be like this?
When will the waiting end?
When will the thoughts finally be dismissed?
Pressure of sobriety.
The pressure of not letting it all get to my head is actually
getting to my head.

But the biggest question is **when** do I draw the line and
stop blaming my childhood?
There was a time when there was damaged created by me
and only me.
The casket had my name on the centerfold.
Nail it shut, even if I scream and shout.
The self-pity and depressing jokes get old.

When do I take the blame?
I must admit that I am as well responsible for my own
corruption.

However—considering my situation,
it's understandable to see how I was blinded by poison.
But I don't want to be toxic to the ones that I love.
I want to put a smile on everyone's face.
But how long will I let this tumor eat away at me?
Infection, sucking its teeth into my bones, decaying.

Losing feelings, discovering new ones.

Learning how to live a healthy life without these
behaviors.
Stability transitioning into actuality.
Wake up calls. Inhale, exhale.
This is a crash course, progress to be made.
It's good enough.

I am good enough.
I am an adult now.
I can do this, I have the control.
Me. No one else. And I will win this battle.
I'm not even half-way there, but at least my eyes are open
now.

Hostage II

One day, you left your castle and I kicked my way free.
It was the most remarkable moment I'll live, honestly.
I ran and I ran, until I felt like my lungs were going to
collapse.
When you get back to your throne, you will see who got
the last laugh.
I'm free. I'm really free at last.

Castle

Come on, sister.
Let's get a wrecking ball, it's demolition day.
Let's tear down the palace and build our own perfect
castle.
Let's build a beautiful fortress.
We can be the king and queen. We can make the rules.
Nothing will matter anymore.

No need to rush anything in fear that life will be cut short.
There are no more custody battles,
no more sitting in the lobby hearing yelling in court.

Drinking bottles and bottles of water,
so the opioids will get out of her system.

We paint the castle my favorite color,
because I whined enough and you gave in.
But let's be honest,
who wants to see a lime green house anyway?

We can hang posters of Missy Higgins and Lana Del Rey.
We can make it bulletproof.
These walls will defeat the big bad wolf.

Our crowns will have tons of glimmering jewels.
We will feel magic in our fingertips.
This entire world will be our kingdom,
a masterpiece that we'll rule over and won't let be
corrupted.

We have standards,
and we will make sure there shall be justice.

We won't lock the door.
We are only afraid of what's not being let into our home,
instead of needing to keep anything out.

Come on sis, what do you say?
Will you save the world with me today?

Not...Again!

It's happening again.
But why? Things are going well and...fuck.
Sometimes I feel like I'm suffocating,
like an elephant is sitting on my chest.
I get so tired of living the same day on repeat.
When will the bullshit be put to rest?
Today I feel like I'm spinning in circles,
but this is an alternate route.
I try to explain how I feel but I can't get the words out.

I feel like I am unfolding,
searching for ways not to feel transparent.
My stomach is churning,
my heart feels like it's about to explode.
But why? Why are my palms beginning to sweat?
Why do I feel this sense of overwhelming?

Oh, it's happening again.
But why? There's nothing wrong.
Oh, no. I'm feeling like a ghost again, drifting along.
Just when I start feeling sane, it's happening again.
I'm attempting to find the answers.
I've never had the opportunity to form the true me,
to create myself the way I intended to be.
My addictive personality soaks it all up.

It's happening again.
Breathe, breathe, breathe.

Relapse

Fuck.
I made a mistake.
But...I got so far.
No no no no no no.
Why did I do that?
I know better! I've worked so hard! Damn it!
I guess…

I'll try again.
I'll just try again.
Start over.

SoberSoberSober

It hasn't been long but I'm sober.
Never thought I could be that strong, but I'm sober.
No more cutting fresh lines on my arms.
I have slowly watched the fading of my scars.
I have thrown away all the chances for a relapse.
I cut out people from my life and wonder if I should have.

I am trying to make a change to better myself.
It's taken a long time for me to realize that I do need help.
I never thought it would happen to someone like me,
but I got caught up in the fantasy of setting myself free.

I told myself only a little bit, but now I know my limits.
I know my limits and don't want to fail.
No need to shred myself up like mail.

Where I've Been

Sometimes I feel like I'm not attached to this world,
or it's as if I am drifting away.
It's as if I'm looking down on the people below,
as they laugh and play.

I try to tell myself that nothing is wrong,
but I give in sometimes.
Sometimes fighting is too much work, so I allow it.
However, I'm more aware now than when I was a kid.

I allow this one to pass as it always does.
I take it minute by minute.
This will pass and soon I'll feel back in my body in the
end.
Connected with this beautiful world and my environment
again.

I might still mess up. I might still crash.
I might still have my bad days which make it hard to get
out of bed, but it'll be worth it.

I can do this.
I may not have reached my best.
But at least it's better than where I've been.

Lost and Found

This is my open apology to all the people I have hurt
while I was hurting.
I felt lost at sea, stranded and the boat was sinking...
I could only distract myself from truth that I tried to deny,
and forget the secrets that I knew.
I lied to myself as if everything I was witnessing and
going through was normal.

I was trying to get through, and there were times when I
was selfish.
A lot of the time I was.
But I had to take care of myself the way no one else did.
My siblings and I all had to fight for ourselves.

I'm sorry for the people I confused,
when I would be present and then fade in the background.
For being so full of life one day and then crash the next.
For making you think that I was a twin that switched
places.

I'm sorry for disappearing for months on end
and then coming back expecting things to be normal.
For needing so much and not enough.
For being desperate for something out of my reach.
I am sorry for being caught up in my storm to not notice
the hurricane around me.
I was only concerned about myself, but I never meant to
cause harm.

And to my ex lovers...

I am sorry for clinging to you for acceptance.
I'm sorry for defining a home in your heart because all my life I've been homeless.

I'm sorry for my insecure spirit and never truly believing anyone cared for me.
I'm sorry that my defenses always get in the way of the joy that life has to offer.

But mostly, this is my apology to myself for losing myself, but as I lost myself for the last time, I truly found myself.
My identity is forming and I'm not a sinking ship.

I am the challenger.

I am a rocket.

       I rise.

             I soar.

PART SIX
progression

Recovery

Recovery isn't a smooth sailing ship.
It's difficult. It's an every day effort.
You will feel amazing, but then you will crash.
You'll have a good week but then a bad day.
It's how it is. It's how it's going to be.
But wouldn't you rather have six good days
And one bad than no days at all?

Identity

You wear your sleeves rolled up to expose your scars.
I could never do that. Not even today.
Does that make me ashamed?
I'm not ashamed. I just don't want to be asked
or judged.
People don't try to understand sometimes.
I also just don't want people to treat me differently.
I am myself.
I am a million other things than a previous cutter.
I am a dog lover.
I am obsessed with tea.
I write my unorganized thoughts.
The family that I do have, I love dearly.
And I am willing to talk about mental illness.
But rolling up my sleeves, even as I wash dishes at work,
I am unable to do that without fear.
Why?

Don't Lose Your Color

Everything changes.
People come in your life and then go,
but please don't lose your color.

I love how innocent you look when you laugh while
watching your favorite TV show.
You eat and some spaghetti sauce drips and you don't
notice it.

Please don't let this world bring you down.
You don't have to bathe in the snow slush.
Your heart is so golden and pure.
It would be a tragedy to see it die so young.

Your simple view of life inspires me to be a better person
and to reevaluate my choices.
I tend to overthink things and overwhelm myself with the
smallest issues.

I remember standing outside of my house with my ex and
hearing how he stopped dreaming.
I said there would never be a day where I wouldn't see a
brighter future full of beautiful pastels.
But at one point I lost my paint.
I lost my brush.
The sky was gray.
I faded in the background within filters.
I lost my color.

But recently, I realized that everything I love now will
eventually be gone.
All those memories and people I held onto for so long.

Oh, but darling, please don't lose your color.
Let yourself be happy and dance for no reason at all.
Don't allow anyone to make you hesitate.
Don't lose yourself along the way.
Your aura is captivating. You light up the room.

But I know it's easier said than done to let the past go.
It lingers with me like a shadow.
It lurks within me, tries to drain my color.
It has succeeded before.

But I've made a comeback.
So please don't discard yourself.
Please don't.
You can do anything.

I couldn't bear to see your heart fade.
Please don't lose your color.

I Can Do This?/Look at Me

Maybe I can't do this, but what if I can?
It's like my demons have a list of demands.
They have their what ifs and pin them up high,
for everyone to see that I have a fucked-up mind.
Suck the life out of me and hang me to dry.
Sometimes I wonder if it's worth the fight.

Because I'm told I'm too depressing.
My poetry needs to be more optimistic.
Well, how can I do that when these feelings are real?
I write about what I know,
and I know that I'm confused and
conflicted about childhood trauma and abuse.

I'm not saying that I'm giving in,
but you need to understand that sometimes
I'm too tired to fight.
I have to rehearse conversations with people that I see,
the weather and did you watch that movie on TV?
I'm surrounded by my demons doubting me,
poking knives and forcing me to bleed.

So just look at me, honey,
and know that I'm trying for the life of me.
Please don't let this be how it ends for me.
I just want to see in color, not in gray.
But I hope to God I'll see better days.
Look at me and you will see.
Someone deeper, deep inside of me.

Unfinished Business

Loving someone passionately, desperately.
Having it end abruptly.
Unfinished business.

Going seventy percent in, and then abandoning a project.
Starting a new novel and fleshing out the story,
but leaving it unfinished.
Unfinished business.

My education.
Unfinished.

My development.
Unfinished.

My interview with a monster.
Unfinished.

We sit parallel, but it's denial of the fittest, not survival.
If the shoe is the right size, then own it.
Coming back home because I thought it would be better
this time around, yet...
How many times will I allow my six-year-old self to come
out?
I'm too old for hide and seek,
Too old to leave work unfinished.

My road to happiness.
I am on my way.

Proud

There was so much that I couldn't control before.
I was terrified that the future would be parallel to all I've
known.
Now I'm aware that I have obtained the power to be able
to let it all go.
I understand now that what happened simply happened,
and there's no point in trying to analyze every detail
anymore.

There was no logic within other people's actions.
So why do I keep sacrificing myself?
Why should I keep protecting you and covering it up?

I am setting myself free. If I don't, then who else will?
I'm proud of myself for realizing that I'm proud of myself
for putting in the effort.

I am done trying to make up for lost time.
I'm so over not forgiving myself when I have nothing to
be sorry for.
I did what I had to do,
so I could make it through.

And I'm proud of myself for coming to terms with that.
I'm proud of myself, and for once
to say that doesn't feel so bad.
I'm proud of myself.

I Won't Apologize

I won't apologize,
For taking care of myself, for running away.
I won't apologize for searching for help, for finding aid.
I found a life worth living.

I don't regret not giving you your millionth chance.
I won't apologize for not playing your game.
I won't apologize because you made me ashamed.

Here's the truth.
I won't apologize to you, for what you put me through,
Things you can't undo.
Is that a hard pill to swallow? Or to snort?
No more custody battles in court,
Because we are at the point of no return.
Consider this as a lesson learned.
I won't apologize for loving myself,
For the very first time in my life.

But I do wish things could've been different.
I'm not angry anymore.
I just feel hope for the future.

I Am Loved

I never have felt comfortable before,
like all my worries were never born.
You show me all the things that I've missed.
Could I be good enough for this?

It's honestly hard to explain how I feel.
It's taken me a while to understand that this is real.
I never thought I would be here now,
but I think I should appreciate the good days.

Moments That Matter

I wish I could freeze moments like these.
They matter more than anything.

Moments that reassure me that I'm not alone.
It's moments like these that mean the most to me.
They remind me that I should be grateful that I breathe all
this fresh air and drink clean water.

I stand tall proud and free.
I can hold my love to my heart safely,
and as we are here together, I couldn't ask for more.
These are the moments that matter.

It's a bittersweet feeling to let go of all that you've lost.
It's an empowering feeling to understand what you've got.

Hold on tight and take off your armor.
No matter what happens, there will not be a casualty.
Don't close yourself off completely,
or you will miss out, you won't see what love can do.
What life is all about, no more pity parties.
You have a lot to be happy for.
Moments that matter most.

More to Life

So, here's this…

I think I need some more time to figure out who I am.

Who I am, what I want, where I want to go, and where I stand.

I worry about living the same old story on repeat.
I know luxuries don't come in a box, formed in love and simplicity.
I fought for so long and crave something more rewarding.
I tell myself to take life as more than just a warning.

The words *or else* are intimidating and make me freeze.
Say the right thing, be careful or they might leave.
Gotten so used to neglect, can't tell when someone's treating me well,
or when they're cruel, so natural, and it's still hard to tell.

What if there is more to life than what I know?
These four walls constructed strong, tight, without a glow.
What if what I think I know isn't true?
But it's my truth,
so don't criticize me for not knowing the latest news.
I am only focused on keeping my two feet on the ground.
Seeing what life has to offer, the landscapes and towns.

We came from two separate worlds and I know mine is strange.

An unfamiliar concept, a thought way out of your limited
range.

Two separate worlds, that you've yet to know.
Two separate worlds, that I'm desperate to let go.

Sure, I've released the toxic people, but how do I know
that history won't repeat itself?
Mother lived in denial, lied to herself days upon days and
never sought out help.
I refuse to end up like that.

I want to see what this life has to offer.
I want to see more.

I want to see the different ways people blink,
how they think, the way they enunciate.
How do they communicate?
What if we are the same?
What if we share a close past?
The same story?
The lack of promise our parents had?
A pure heart like me.

Seven billion people out in this world with a perspective
not like our own.
There's got to be more to life than this.
The whole – go to work – go home – eat – go to sleep.

There has to be more to life than what I've seen.
Hiding behind furniture, scream!
Watching fists --kiss--- swollen lips, I'm gonna leave!
There's got to be more.

Like a whole new opinion on why we are all here.
Theories to explore our smallest fears.

Studies to expose our hearts to coldest of people and help
them warm up.

There has to be more to life than dreading.
Than washing the bedding after my dog got sick.
Letting ourselves sink into rehearsed patterns through
clear cups.

There has to be more to life than paychecks spent on
cheap liquor to cleanse ourselves, and to scrape off sad
tendencies like how we miss her.

We say goodbye to fears that burns inside us,
and make us fear our own fearful selves that only gives us
night terrors.
We strive to break the cycle.

There has to be more to life than eating the same food.
Not diversifying, breaking routines, dumping out the
booze, too tired so you keep hitting snooze,
because you're too depressed to wake up before noon.
Using cover up to hide your husband's new bruise
that he caused because you got water on the floor.

There's got to be more to life than this.

I know because I have seen great things,
and I've only been living since I was a little over nineteen,
that's five years now and in the making.
I thought this would only be a dream.
That's all I thought it'd be, for me.

You can make your life into a trophy life.
~~but only if you do it right.~~
Actually, scratch that.
You can fuck up and you just might,

that's all right.

So go wake up before anyone else does.
Drink some Summer Rose tea.
Join me.
Watch the sunrise, and we gaze at the same sky, you'll see.
You will find yourself and gain a piece of dignity,
and celebrate life and all that you need
to be, all that you need to achieve.
See things you once believed are at last within your reach.

There **IS** more to life than fragile identities and
living in purgatory.
So allow yourself to take a leave of absence,
and make choices to license yourself permission to...
JUST BE FUCKING FREE!!!

But only you can be to do that, all right?
How crazy is it that your future and destiny rest in your
hands?

Even if you crawled out of the depths of hell,
just know that I have done the same and am now seeing
my dog wag her tail…
and I don't feel as if I have failed.

You and I both will find that we can imagine and
appreciate the finest things.

No limitations, no restrictions.
Just realize there's more to life than the shit you were
handed as a little kid.
It's not your fault for what they did.
Take some action.
No more negative reactions.
There's more to you than that.

And there's more to life than this.
There's more to life than this.
There's so much more, so much more.

So. Much. More.

<u>My Gratitude:</u>

I just wanted to say thank you to all of the people that believed in me before I believed in myself. It's been a long journey to feel good about myself. Thank you.

Jason – thank you being realistic and putting me back down to earth when I need it.

Tiffany – thank you for being the best big sister anyone can dream of. For being a true friend.

Jared – thank you for showing what a normal life could be for people like us. You excel and continue on with life.

Kaycee – for being an amazing friend during the darkest period of my life and still being a fellow person who struggles. Larvae for life <3

TJ – thank you for helping me edit! I truly appreciate what you've done to help me! You're wonderful!

To those at the hospital with me – you have all changed my life so much. Thank you for being a missing piece in my heart. Thank you for showing me that I'm not alone. Thank you for treating me like a human and for loving me even with all of my scars.

And if I don't write your name on here...that doesn't mean that I am not thankful for all of the people that I have met in my life. Every person that has entered and left or faded in the background has left a mark on my heart and I cherish every lesson that each and every one of you has taught me.

Helplines:

US Suicide Prevention Lifeline
1-800-273-8255

Crisis Chat or Crisis Text Line
Text HOME to 741741

Depression and Bipolar Alliance Hotline – Support Group
1-800-826-3632

Suicide Prevention Services Crisis Hotline
1-800-784-2433

Suicide Prevention Services Depression Hotline
1-630-482-9696

Child Abuse Hotline – Support & Information
1-800-422-4453

Crisis Help Hotline – For Any Kind of Crisis
1-800-233-4357

Domestic & Teen Dating Violence (English & Spanish)
1-800-992-2600

Parental Stress Hotline – Help for Parents
1-800-632-8188

Runaway Hotline
1-800-231-6946

Sexual Assault Hotline (24/7, English & Spanish)
1-800-223-5001

Crisis and Homeless Help Hotline –Covenant House
1-800-999-9999

National Child Abuse Hotline
1-800-422-4453

National Domestic Violence Hotline
1-800-799-7233

National Youth Crisis Hotline
1-800-448-4663

Please take care.

Printed in Great Britain
by Amazon